THE THRIVING VISION

Charting the Path to Sustainable Business Success

NANCY BARLOW

Copyright © 2024 by Nancy Barlow

All rights reserved. No part of this book may be reproduced, stored in a retrieval system, or transmitted, in any form or by any means, electronic, mechanical, photocopying, recording, or otherwise, without the prior written permission of the author, except in the case of brief quotations embodied in critical reviews and certain other noncommercial uses permitted by copyright law.

TABLE OF CONTENT

INTRODUCTION 5

CHAPTER 1: THE EVOLUTION OF BUSINESS: FROM PROFIT TO PURPOSE 8

- Understanding the Shift Towards Sustainable Business Practices 10

- Historical Context and Milestones in the Sustainability Movement 16

- The Business Case for Sustainability: Why it Pays to Prioritize Purpose 23

CHAPTER 2: THE PILLARS OF SUSTAINABLE SUCCESS 29

- Environmental Stewardship: Navigating the Challenges of Climate Change and Resource Scarcity 31

- Social Responsibility: Building Strong Communities and Promoting Equity 38

- Economic Resilience: Balancing Profitability with Long-Term Stability 44

Chapter 3: Strategies for Integrating Sustainability into Business Models 50

- Reimagining Supply Chains: From Linear to Circular Economies 53

- Innovating for Sustainability: Harnessing Technology and Creativity 59

- Engaging Stakeholders: Building Trust and Collaboration 66

CHAPTER 4: CULTIVATING A PURPOSE-DRIVEN CULTURE 74

- Leadership in the Age of Sustainability: Inspiring Vision and Driving Change 76

- Fostering Employee Engagement: Empowering Teams and Nurturing Talent 82

- Ethical Governance: Setting Standards and Upholding Integrity 88

CHAPTER 5: NAVIGATING THE FUTURE OF SUSTAINABLE BUSINESS 95

- Anticipating Trends and Disruptions: The Role of Scenario Planning 98

- Scaling Impact: From Local Initiatives to Global Movements 104

CONCLUSION 111

INTRODUCTION

In the pulsating heart of the business world, where innovation meets necessity, and aspiration dances with pragmatism, lies the essence of sustainable success. In "The Thriving Vision: Charting the Path to Sustainable Business Success," we embark on a journey that transcends conventional wisdom, delving into the realm where profitability intertwines with purpose, and where longevity is born from a harmonious balance between progress and preservation.

Today's landscape of commerce is marked by a profound shift—a shift towards sustainability, where businesses are increasingly called upon to not only deliver value to shareholders but also to embrace their responsibilities to society and the environment. This evolution isn't merely a trend; it's a fundamental restructuring of the very fabric of business, one that demands a new approach, a new mindset, and a new vision.

Within the pages of this book, we illuminate the pathways that lead not just to success, but to enduring prosperity. We challenge the notion that profitability and sustainability are at odds, presenting a compelling argument that they are, in fact, mutually reinforcing. Drawing upon insights from pioneering companies, visionary leaders, and cutting-edge research, we unveil the principles and practices that underpin sustainable business success.

"The Thriving Vision" isn't just about theory—it's a practical guide for leaders and entrepreneurs who are ready to embrace the future of business. From reimagining business models to fostering innovation, from cultivating purpose-driven cultures to navigating the complexities of stakeholder relationships, this book equips readers with the tools, strategies, and mindset needed to thrive in an ever-changing world.

But this book is more than just a roadmap—it's a call to action. It's a call to transcend the status quo and embrace a new paradigm of business—one that is built not just for today, but for generations to come. It's a call to harness the power of enterprise for the betterment of society and the preservation of our planet.

As we embark on this journey together, let us not only chart a path to sustainable business success but also ignite a movement—a movement that transforms the way we do business, the way we interact with our world, and the way we envision the future. Let "The Thriving Vision" be our compass, guiding us towards a future where prosperity is measured not just in profit, but in the profound and lasting impact we create.

Welcome to "The Thriving Vision"—where the pursuit of success meets the imperative of sustainability, and where the possibilities for a brighter future are limited only by our collective imagination.

CHAPTER 1: THE EVOLUTION OF BUSINESS: FROM PROFIT TO PURPOSE

In the annals of economic history, the evolution of business reflects not only the changing dynamics of commerce but also the shifting values and aspirations of society. From the industrial revolution to the digital age, businesses have been shaped by a multitude of forces—from technological advancements to geopolitical shifts. Yet, perhaps one of the most transformative developments in recent times is the ascendancy of purpose alongside profit.

In this chapter, we embark on a journey through time—a journey that illuminates the profound evolution of business from a singular focus on profit to an embrace of broader societal and environmental responsibilities. We explore the catalysts behind this paradigm shift, the key milestones that have marked its progression, and the compelling reasons why purpose-driven business practices have emerged as imperative in the modern era.

But this isn't merely a historical account—it's a narrative that unfolds against the backdrop of a world grappling with pressing challenges, from climate change to social inequality. It's a narrative that underscores the interconnectedness of business with the wider tapestry of society, and the recognition that the pursuit of profit must be reconciled with the imperative of purpose.

As we delve into the evolution of business, we confront fundamental questions: What sparked the transition from profit-centric to purpose-driven paradigms? How have businesses responded to changing societal expectations? And what does the future hold for this ongoing transformation?

Join us as we unravel the threads of history, exploring how businesses have navigated the complex terrain of profit and purpose, and charting a course towards a future where success is measured not just in financial terms, but in the positive impact we create for people and the planet. Welcome to the evolution of business—from profit to purpose.

- Understanding the Shift Towards Sustainable Business Practices

In recent years, there has been a significant shift in the way businesses perceive and approach sustainability. Once viewed primarily as a niche concern or a mere regulatory obligation, sustainability has now emerged as a strategic imperative for companies across industries. This shift reflects a growing recognition of the interconnectedness between business operations, environmental stewardship, social responsibility, and long-term economic viability. In this discussion, we will explore the factors driving this shift, the key principles underpinning sustainable business practices, and the implications for organizations striving to thrive in a rapidly changing world.

Drivers of Change:

Several interconnected factors have contributed to the momentum behind the shift towards sustainable business practices:

1. **Growing Environmental Concerns:** Increasing awareness of environmental issues such as climate change, resource depletion, pollution, and biodiversity loss has led to heightened public scrutiny and demand for action. Businesses are facing mounting pressure to minimize their ecological footprint and adopt more sustainable production and consumption patterns.

2. **Social and Ethical Considerations:** There is a growing emphasis on corporate social responsibility (CSR) and ethical business conduct. Stakeholders, including consumers, investors, employees, and

communities, are demanding greater transparency, accountability, and ethical behavior from companies. Issues such as labor rights, human rights, diversity, and fair trade have become central concerns for businesses seeking to build trust and maintain their social license to operate.

3. **Economic Imperatives:** Sustainability is increasingly recognized as a source of competitive advantage and business resilience. Companies that proactively address environmental and social risks can mitigate operational disruptions, reduce costs, enhance brand reputation, and access new markets and investment opportunities. Moreover, evolving regulatory frameworks and market dynamics are incentivizing businesses to adopt more sustainable practices to remain compliant and competitive in the long term.

Principles of Sustainable Business Practices:

Sustainable business practices are guided by a set of core principles that encompass environmental, social, and economic dimensions:

1. **Triple Bottom Line:** Sustainable businesses seek to optimize outcomes across three interconnected dimensions: people, planet, and profit. This triple bottom-line approach recognizes that economic success should not come at the expense of social well-being or environmental integrity.

2. **Lifecycle Thinking:** Sustainability entails considering the entire lifecycle of products and services, from raw material extraction to disposal or recycling. Businesses aim to minimize resource use, waste generation, and environmental impacts throughout the product lifecycle, adopting principles of eco-design, resource efficiency, and circular economy.

3. **Stakeholder Engagement:** Sustainable businesses actively engage with stakeholders to understand their diverse interests, concerns, and expectations. By fostering transparent communication, collaboration, and dialogue with stakeholders, companies can build trust, address societal needs, and co-create value for all parties involved.

4. **Continuous Improvement:** Sustainability is a journey of continuous improvement, requiring ongoing innovation, learning, and adaptation. Businesses set ambitious goals, measure performance against key indicators, and strive for incremental progress over time. They embrace a culture of innovation, experimentation, and resilience to navigate complex challenges and seize emerging opportunities.

Implications for Organizations:

For organizations seeking to embrace sustainable business practices, there are several critical implications to consider:

1. **Strategic Alignment:** Sustainability should be integrated into the core strategy, values, and operations of the organization, rather than treated as a peripheral issue or standalone initiative. Leaders must articulate a clear vision, set ambitious goals, and allocate resources effectively to drive meaningful change.

2. **Cross-functional collaboration:** Achieving sustainability requires collaboration across departments, functions, and stakeholders within and beyond the organization. Effective cross-functional teamwork, supported by strong leadership, communication, and governance mechanisms, is essential to align diverse interests, leverage expertise, and drive collective action.

3. **Risk Management:** Businesses must proactively identify, assess, and manage environmental, social, and governance (ESG) risks and opportunities across their value chain. By conducting comprehensive risk assessments, implementing robust management systems, and embedding resilience into their operations, organizations can enhance their ability to anticipate and respond to evolving sustainability challenges.

4. **Innovation and Adaptation:** Sustainability presents opportunities for innovation, differentiation, and competitive advantage. Organizations that embrace a culture of innovation, agility, and experimentation can develop new

products, services, and business models that meet evolving customer needs, regulatory requirements, and societal expectations.

In conclusion, the shift towards sustainable business practices represents a fundamental transformation in the way organizations conceptualize and conduct business. By embracing sustainability as a strategic imperative, guided by principles of environmental stewardship, social responsibility, and economic resilience, businesses can create value for society, foster long-term prosperity, and contribute to a more sustainable and inclusive future for all.

- Historical Context and Milestones in the Sustainability Movement

The sustainability movement has deep roots, stretching back over centuries, but it gained significant traction in the latter half of the 20th century and has since evolved into a global phenomenon. Understanding the historical context and key milestones in the sustainability movement provides valuable insights into the progression of environmental awareness, social activism, and corporate responsibility over time. In this comprehensive discussion, we will explore the historical context of sustainability, highlight key milestones in its development, and examine the influential events, initiatives, and movements that have shaped the modern sustainability landscape.

Historical Context:

The roots of the sustainability movement can be traced back to various historical, cultural, and philosophical influences, including indigenous wisdom, religious teachings, and environmental conservation movements. Concepts such as stewardship of the Earth, reverence for nature, and the interconnectedness of all living beings have been central tenets of indigenous cultures for millennia, providing a foundation for modern sustainability principles.

The Industrial Revolution of the 18th and 19th centuries marked a pivotal moment in human history, ushering in an era of unprecedented economic growth, technological innovation, and urbanization. However, it also brought about profound environmental degradation, social inequalities, and exploitation of natural resources. The adverse impacts of industrialization, combined with the emergence of scientific theories on ecology and environmentalism, sparked early concerns about the finite limits of the Earth's resources and the need for sustainable development.

Key Milestones:

1. **Early Conservation Movements:** The late 19th and early 20th centuries saw the emergence of conservation movements aimed at preserving natural landscapes, wildlife habitats, and cultural heritage sites. Influential figures such as John Muir, Theodore Roosevelt, and Aldo Leopold played instrumental roles in advocating for the protection of wilderness areas, the establishment of national parks, and the conservation of biodiversity.

2. **Environmental Awareness in the 1960s and 1970s:** The 1960s and 1970s witnessed a surge of environmental activism and awareness, fueled by growing concerns about pollution, deforestation, and the impacts of industrialization on human health and the environment. The publication of Rachel Carson's groundbreaking book "Silent Spring" in 1962, which exposed the dangers of pesticides such as DDT, galvanized public support for environmental conservation and regulatory action.

3. **The United Nations and Global Environmental Governance:** The United Nations played a central role in elevating environmental issues on the global agenda, leading to the establishment of key institutions and agreements aimed at addressing environmental challenges. The United Nations Conference on the Human Environment, held in Stockholm in 1972, marked the first international gathering focused on environmental issues and laid the groundwork for

subsequent efforts to promote sustainable development.

4. The Brundtland Report and the Concept of Sustainable Development: In 1987, the World Commission on Environment and Development, chaired by former Norwegian Prime Minister Gro Harlem Brundtland, published the landmark report "Our Common Future." This report popularized the concept of sustainable development, defining it as "development that meets the needs of the present without compromising the ability of future generations to meet their own needs." The Brundtland Report helped mainstream sustainability as a guiding principle for global policymaking and development strategies.

5. Corporate Sustainability Initiatives: In the late 20th and early 21st centuries, an increasing number of businesses began to recognize the importance of sustainability in their operations and supply chains. Companies started adopting corporate social responsibility (CSR) practices, integrating environmental and social considerations into their business strategies, and engaging with stakeholders to address sustainability challenges. Initiatives such as the Global Reporting Initiative (GRI) and the formation of sustainability-focused industry associations helped drive the adoption of responsible business practices and transparency in reporting.

6. **Rise of the Green Economy and Sustainable Investing:** The 21st century has witnessed the emergence of the green economy—a transition towards economic activities that promote environmental sustainability, resource efficiency, and social equity. Sustainable investing, which considers environmental, social, and governance (ESG) factors alongside financial returns, has gained momentum as investors seek to align their portfolios with sustainability objectives and mitigate long-term risks.

Implications and Future Directions:

The historical context and milestones in the sustainability movement highlight the evolution of environmental awareness, social activism, and corporate responsibility over time. While progress has been made in addressing environmental and social challenges, significant gaps and obstacles remain, including climate change, biodiversity loss, social inequality, and unsustainable consumption patterns.

Looking ahead, the sustainability movement faces complex and interconnected challenges that require collective action, innovative solutions, and transformative change at local, national, and global levels. Achieving sustainability will require collaboration across sectors, disciplines, and borders, as well as a commitment to equity, justice, and inclusivity. By building on the legacy of past achievements, embracing new opportunities for collaboration and innovation, and reimagining our relationship with the natural world, we can chart a course towards a more sustainable and resilient future for all.

- The Business Case for Sustainability: Why it Pays to Prioritize Purpose

Sustainability has transcended its origins as a moral imperative or regulatory compliance requirement to become a strategic necessity for businesses worldwide. Increasingly, companies are recognizing that integrating sustainability into their operations not only aligns with societal and environmental goals but also delivers tangible benefits to their bottom line and long-term competitiveness. In this comprehensive discussion, we will explore the compelling business case for sustainability, examining the economic, operational, reputational, and strategic advantages that accrue to organizations that prioritize purpose and responsible business practices.

1. **Cost Savings and Efficiency Gains:**

   - Sustainability initiatives often lead to significant cost savings through increased efficiency in resource use, waste reduction, and energy conservation.

   - Investments in energy-efficient technologies, renewable energy sources, and sustainable supply chain practices can lower operational expenses and enhance profitability over time.

   - By optimizing resource utilization and minimizing waste generation, companies can achieve greater productivity, improve asset utilization, and reduce their environmental footprint.

2. **Risk Mitigation and Resilience:**

   - Embracing sustainability helps companies mitigate various environmental, social, and governance (ESG) risks, including regulatory compliance, supply chain disruptions, reputational damage, and financial liabilities.

- By proactively addressing sustainability challenges such as climate change, water scarcity, and social inequality, organizations can enhance their resilience to external shocks and future-proof their business operations.

- Investors and stakeholders are increasingly scrutinizing companies' ESG performance as a measure of risk management and long-term value creation, making sustainability a critical factor in investment decisions and access to capital.

3. Market Differentiation and Competitive Advantage:

- Sustainability can serve as a powerful driver of market differentiation, enabling companies to distinguish themselves from competitors, attract customers, and capture new market opportunities.

- Consumers are increasingly seeking products and services that align with their values and environmental concerns, driving demand for sustainable brands and driving market growth.

- Companies that demonstrate a commitment to sustainability can enhance their brand reputation, build customer loyalty, and foster trust among stakeholders, thereby gaining a competitive edge in the marketplace.

4. Innovation and Business Opportunities:

- Sustainability challenges present opportunities for innovation, creativity, and entrepreneurship, driving the development of new products, services, and business models.

- Companies that invest in sustainable innovation can create disruptive technologies, enter new markets, and unlock untapped revenue streams while addressing societal and environmental needs.

- Collaborative partnerships with stakeholders, including suppliers, customers, and research institutions, can facilitate knowledge sharing, technology transfer, and co-innovation to address complex sustainability challenges.

5. Talent Attraction and Retention:

- Embracing sustainability enhances employee engagement, morale, and satisfaction by aligning organizational values with individual aspirations and societal goals.

- Millennials and Gen Z, who constitute a significant portion of the workforce, prioritize purpose-driven work environments and seek employers that demonstrate a commitment to sustainability and social responsibility.

- Companies that foster a culture of sustainability, diversity, and inclusion can attract top talent, retain skilled employees, and drive innovation through diverse perspectives and experiences.

In conclusion, the business case for sustainability is compelling and multifaceted, encompassing economic, operational, reputational, and strategic benefits for organizations of all sizes and sectors. By prioritizing purpose and integrating sustainability into their business strategies, companies can achieve cost savings, mitigate risks, differentiate themselves in the marketplace, drive innovation, attract talent, and create long-term value for shareholders and stakeholders alike. Ultimately, sustainability is not just a moral imperative—it is a smart business decision that pays dividends in the pursuit of a more prosperous, equitable, and resilient future for all.

CHAPTER 2: THE PILLARS OF SUSTAINABLE SUCCESS

In the dynamic landscape of business, success is no longer defined solely by financial metrics or short-term gains. Instead, it is increasingly measured by a company's ability to thrive in harmony with the planet, its people, and its profits. This fundamental shift has given rise to the concept of sustainable success—a holistic approach that recognizes the interconnectedness of environmental stewardship, social responsibility, and economic resilience.

In this chapter, we delve into the pillars that form the foundation of sustainable success, exploring the essential principles and practices that enable organizations to flourish in a rapidly changing world. From environmental sustainability to social equity to economic viability, each pillar plays a crucial role in shaping the sustainable business practices of today and the resilient enterprises of tomorrow.

As we navigate through the pillars of sustainable success, we will uncover the strategies, innovations, and collaborations that drive positive impact and create value for all stakeholders. We will examine how leading organizations integrate sustainability into their core operations, foster inclusive cultures, and navigate complex challenges to achieve enduring prosperity.

But this chapter is more than just a theoretical exploration—it is a practical guide for businesses seeking to embrace sustainability as a strategic imperative. Through real-world examples, case studies, and best practices, we will illustrate how companies across industries are harnessing the power of sustainability to drive innovation, mitigate risks, and unlock new growth opportunities.

As we embark on this journey through the pillars of sustainable success, let us envision a future where business thrives not at the expense of the planet or its people, but in harmony with them. Let us challenge the status quo, inspire change, and build a more sustainable, equitable, and prosperous world for generations to come. Welcome to "The Pillars of Sustainable Success"—where purpose meets profit, and where the possibilities for a brighter future are limited only by our collective imagination.

- Environmental Stewardship: Navigating the Challenges of Climate Change and Resource Scarcity

Environmental Stewardship: Navigating the Challenges of Climate Change and Resource Scarcity

Environmental stewardship is a cornerstone of sustainable business practices, encompassing efforts to minimize ecological impacts, preserve natural resources, and mitigate climate change. In today's rapidly changing world, businesses face mounting pressures to address environmental challenges such as climate change, resource scarcity, pollution, and biodiversity loss. Navigating these challenges requires a proactive approach to environmental stewardship that integrates sustainability principles into all aspects of business operations, from supply chain management to product design to energy consumption. In this comprehensive discussion, we will explore the complex issues surrounding environmental stewardship, examine the impacts of climate change and resource scarcity on businesses, and identify strategies for building resilience and driving positive change.

1. **Climate Change:**

Climate change poses one of the most significant threats to the planet's ecosystems, economies, and societies. Rising temperatures, extreme weather events, shifting precipitation patterns, and sea-level rise are already having profound impacts on businesses worldwide. The consequences of climate change, including disruptions to supply chains, increased operational risks, regulatory pressures, and reputational damage, are forcing companies to rethink their approach to environmental stewardship.

Strategies for addressing climate change include:

- Setting science-based emissions reduction targets to align with the goals of the Paris Agreement.

- Investing in renewable energy sources, energy efficiency measures, and low-carbon technologies to reduce greenhouse gas emissions.

- Implementing climate risk assessments and resilience planning to anticipate and mitigate the impacts of climate-related hazards.

- Engaging with stakeholders, including investors, customers, and communities, to promote climate action and transparency in reporting.

2. **Resource Scarcity:**

Resource scarcity, including water scarcity, land degradation, and depletion of natural resources, poses significant challenges to businesses operating in resource-intensive industries. As populations grow, consumption patterns change and ecosystems degrade, the availability and affordability of key resources are increasingly under pressure. Businesses must adopt strategies to minimize resource use, optimize resource efficiency, and promote circular economy principles to reduce waste and maximize resource recovery.

Strategies for addressing resource scarcity include:

- Conducting lifecycle assessments to identify opportunities for resource optimization and waste reduction throughout the value chain.

- Implementing sustainable sourcing practices, including responsible procurement of raw materials and adoption of sustainable agricultural practices.

- Investing in innovative technologies, such as water recycling systems, waste-to-energy solutions, and closed-loop manufacturing processes, to minimize resource consumption and environmental impact.

- Collaborating with suppliers, industry partners, and policymakers to promote sustainable resource management practices and address systemic challenges related to resource scarcity.

3. **Integration of Environmental Stewardship into Business Strategy:**

Environmental stewardship must be integrated into the core strategy, values, and operations of businesses to achieve meaningful and lasting impact. Companies can no longer afford to view sustainability as a peripheral issue or standalone initiative—it must be embedded into decision-making processes, governance structures, and performance metrics. By embracing environmental stewardship as a strategic imperative, businesses can unlock opportunities for innovation, differentiation, and long-term value creation while contributing to the preservation of the planet and its resources.

Strategies for integrating environmental stewardship into business strategy include:

- Establishing sustainability goals and targets that align with the organization's mission, values, and stakeholders' expectations.

- Embedding sustainability considerations into product design, manufacturing processes, and supply chain management practices to minimize environmental impacts.

- Engaging employees, customers, and other stakeholders in sustainability initiatives through education, awareness-building, and collaboration.

- Monitoring and reporting on environmental performance metrics, including carbon emissions, water usage, waste generation, and biodiversity impacts, to track progress and demonstrate accountability.

In conclusion, environmental stewardship is a critical component of sustainable business practices, requiring proactive efforts to address the challenges of climate change and resource scarcity. By embracing strategies for reducing greenhouse gas emissions, minimizing resource consumption, and integrating sustainability into business strategy, companies can build resilience, drive innovation, and contribute to a more sustainable future for generations to come. Environmental stewardship is not only a moral imperative—it is also a strategic imperative that pays dividends in terms of risk mitigation, cost savings, and competitive advantage. As businesses navigate the complex landscape of environmental challenges, they have an opportunity to lead by example, inspire change, and create a positive impact for the planet and its inhabitants.

- Social Responsibility: Building Strong Communities and Promoting Equity

Social responsibility is a foundational pillar of sustainable business practices, emphasizing a company's commitment to contributing positively to society and promoting equity, inclusivity, and well-being. In today's interconnected world, businesses are increasingly expected to go beyond profit generation and actively engage with stakeholders to address social challenges, improve quality of life, and create shared value for communities. In this comprehensive discussion, we will explore the multifaceted dimensions of social responsibility, examine the importance of building strong communities and promoting equity, and identify strategies for businesses to integrate social responsibility into their operations and culture.

1. **Building Strong Communities:**

Strong communities are essential for fostering social cohesion, resilience, and economic prosperity. Businesses have a unique opportunity—and responsibility—to contribute to the vitality and well-being of the communities in which they operate. This involves more than philanthropy or corporate giving; it requires meaningful engagement, collaboration, and investment in initiatives that address local needs and priorities.

Strategies for building strong communities include:

- Establishing partnerships with community organizations, nonprofits, and local government agencies to address pressing social issues, such as education, healthcare, affordable housing, and workforce development.

- Supporting small businesses, entrepreneurs, and local suppliers through procurement practices, mentorship programs, and access to capital.

- Investing in infrastructure, public amenities, and cultural institutions that enhance the quality of life and social capital within communities.

- Engaging employees in volunteerism, community service projects, and civic engagement activities to foster a sense of belonging and connection to the communities they serve.

2. **Promoting Equity and Inclusivity:**

Promoting equity and inclusivity is essential for creating a fair and just society where everyone has equal opportunities to thrive. Businesses play a critical role in advancing diversity, equity, and inclusion (DEI) both within their organizations and in the broader society. This involves addressing systemic barriers, biases, and inequalities that perpetuate social injustice and exclusion.

Strategies for promoting equity and inclusivity include:

- Implementing diversity and inclusion policies, training programs, and recruitment practices to attract, retain, and advance a diverse workforce that reflects the communities they serve.

- Ensuring pay equity, providing fair wages, and offering opportunities for career advancement and professional development for all employees, regardless of race, gender, ethnicity, sexual orientation, or socioeconomic background.

- Creating inclusive work environments that value and celebrate diversity, foster belongingness, and encourage open dialogue and mutual respect.

- Supporting marginalized and underrepresented groups through targeted initiatives, scholarships, mentorship programs, and supplier diversity efforts to promote economic empowerment and social mobility.

3. **Stakeholder Engagement and Collaboration:**

Effective social responsibility requires meaningful engagement and collaboration with a wide range of stakeholders, including employees, customers, suppliers, communities, civil society organizations, and government agencies. By listening to diverse perspectives, understanding stakeholder needs, and building collaborative partnerships, businesses can co-create solutions to complex social challenges and drive positive change.

Strategies for stakeholder engagement and collaboration include:

- Establishing formal mechanisms for dialogue, feedback, and consultation with stakeholders to inform decision-making, strategy development, and performance evaluation.

- Participating in multi-stakeholder initiatives, industry collaborations, and collective impact efforts that address systemic social issues and leverage collective resources and expertise.

- Integrating stakeholder perspectives into product development, marketing strategies, and business practices to ensure alignment with societal values and preferences.

- Advocating for public policies and regulatory frameworks that promote social justice, human rights, and sustainable development at local, national, and global levels.

In conclusion, social responsibility is an integral aspect of sustainable business practices, emphasizing the importance of building strong communities, promoting equity, and fostering inclusivity. By embracing strategies for community engagement, diversity and inclusion, and stakeholder collaboration, businesses can create shared value, enhance their reputation, and contribute to a more equitable and sustainable world. Social responsibility is not only a moral imperative—it is also a strategic imperative that drives innovation, resilience, and long-term success. As businesses navigate the complex landscape of social challenges, they have an opportunity to lead by example, inspire change, and make a meaningful difference in the lives of individuals and communities around the globe.

- Economic Resilience: Balancing Profitability with Long-Term Stability

Economic resilience is a critical aspect of sustainable business practices, emphasizing the need for businesses to balance short-term profitability with long-term stability and prosperity. In today's volatile and uncertain economic environment, characterized by rapid technological advancements, global market disruptions, and complex geopolitical dynamics, businesses face a myriad of challenges that threaten their financial viability and competitiveness. Economic resilience entails building adaptive capacity, flexibility, and strategic foresight to withstand shocks, seize opportunities, and thrive in a dynamic and evolving marketplace. In this comprehensive discussion, we will explore the multifaceted dimensions of economic resilience, examine the importance of balancing profitability with long-term stability, and identify strategies for businesses to enhance their economic resilience and ensure sustainable growth.

1. Balancing Short-Term Profitability with Long-Term Stability:

Achieving economic resilience requires striking a delicate balance between maximizing short-term profits and safeguarding long-term value creation. While profitability is essential for business survival and growth, excessive focus on short-term gains at the expense of long-term sustainability can undermine resilience and erode stakeholder trust. Businesses must adopt a holistic approach to decision-making that considers the impacts of their actions on financial performance, reputation, and societal well-being over time.

Strategies for balancing profitability with long-term stability include:

- Aligning financial goals with broader sustainability objectives, such as environmental stewardship, social responsibility, and ethical governance, to create shared value for stakeholders.

- Investing in strategic initiatives, research and development, and capacity-building activities that enhance long-term competitiveness and innovation capabilities.

- Diversifying revenue streams, customer segments, and geographic markets to reduce dependence on volatile or declining sectors and mitigate market risks.

- Cultivating a culture of financial prudence, risk management, and resilience planning that emphasizes transparency, accountability, and ethical conduct.

2. **Embracing Innovation and Adaptation:**

Economic resilience relies on the ability of businesses to innovate, adapt, and evolve in response to changing market conditions, technological disruptions, and consumer preferences. Innovation is not just about developing new products or services—it's also about finding novel solutions to emerging challenges, optimizing business processes, and leveraging digital technologies to enhance efficiency and agility.

Strategies for embracing innovation and adaptation include:

- Investing in research and development, technology adoption, and digital transformation initiatives to drive innovation and enhance operational efficiency.

- Fostering a culture of creativity, experimentation, and continuous improvement that encourages employees to challenge the status quo, embrace change, and learn from failures.

- Collaborating with external partners, including startups, academia, and industry peers, to access new ideas, expertise, and resources and accelerate innovation cycles.

- Monitoring market trends, customer feedback, and competitive intelligence to identify emerging opportunities and pivot strategies accordingly.

3. Strengthening Supply Chain Resilience:

Supply chain disruptions can have significant economic consequences, impacting production schedules, distribution channels, and customer satisfaction. Building supply chain resilience involves diversifying suppliers, reducing dependencies, and proactively managing risks to ensure continuity of operations and minimize disruptions.

Strategies for strengthening supply chain resilience include:

- Mapping supply chain networks, identifying critical dependencies, and assessing vulnerabilities to natural disasters, geopolitical instability, and other external shocks.

- Establishing redundant sourcing options, alternative logistics routes, and inventory buffers to mitigate supply chain risks and maintain business continuity.

- Collaborating with suppliers, logistics providers, and other stakeholders to share information, coordinate response efforts, and build collective resilience.

- Implementing advanced technologies, such as blockchain, artificial intelligence, and Internet of Things (IoT), to enhance supply chain visibility, traceability, and responsiveness.

In conclusion, economic resilience is essential for businesses to thrive in an increasingly complex and volatile economic landscape. By balancing short-term profitability with long-term stability, embracing innovation and adaptation, and strengthening supply chain resilience, businesses can enhance their capacity to withstand shocks, seize opportunities, and achieve sustainable growth. Economic resilience is not just about weathering storms—it's about building the foundations for long-term success, resilience, and prosperity in a dynamic and uncertain world. As businesses navigate the evolving economic challenges, they have an opportunity to demonstrate leadership, resilience, and foresight, driving positive change and creating value for stakeholders across the globe.

Chapter 3: Strategies for Integrating Sustainability into Business Models

In the ever-evolving landscape of commerce, sustainability has emerged as a defining imperative for businesses seeking to thrive in the 21st century. No longer relegated to the realm of corporate social responsibility reports or philanthropic gestures, sustainability has become a strategic imperative that drives innovation, resilience, and long-term value creation. In this chapter, we explore the strategies for integrating sustainability into business models, examining how organizations can reimagine their operations, products, and services to align with environmental, social, and economic sustainability goals.

As the global community grapples with pressing challenges such as climate change, resource scarcity, social inequality, and economic volatility, businesses are increasingly recognizing the need to adopt more sustainable practices that mitigate risks, enhance resilience, and create shared value for all stakeholders. From rethinking supply chains to redesigning products, from fostering inclusive cultures to embracing circular economy principles, there are myriad opportunities for businesses to embed sustainability into their DNA and drive positive impact.

In this chapter, we will delve into the strategies and best practices that enable organizations to integrate sustainability into their business models effectively. Drawing upon insights from pioneering companies, thought leaders, and sustainability experts, we will explore practical approaches for navigating the complexities of sustainability, overcoming barriers to change, and unlocking new opportunities for growth and innovation.

Whether you're a multinational corporation or a small startup, whether you operate in manufacturing, finance, technology, or retail, the principles of sustainability are relevant and applicable to businesses of all sizes and sectors. By embracing sustainability as a strategic imperative and adopting a holistic approach to business model innovation, organizations can not only future-proof their operations but also contribute to a more sustainable, equitable, and prosperous world for generations to come.

Join us as we explore the strategies for integrating sustainability into business models and embark on a journey towards a future where purpose and profit converge, and where sustainability is not just a goal to be achieved, but a way of doing business that benefits people, the planet, and prosperity. Welcome to "Strategies for Integrating Sustainability into Business Models"—where the pursuit of sustainability meets the imperative of success.

- Reimagining Supply Chains: From Linear to Circular Economies

Supply chains form the backbone of modern commerce, facilitating the flow of goods, services, and information across global networks. However, traditional linear supply chains, characterized by a "take-make-dispose" model, are inherently wasteful, inefficient, and environmentally unsustainable. In contrast, circular economies offer a paradigm shift towards a regenerative, closed-loop approach that aims to minimize waste, conserve resources, and maximize the value of products throughout their lifecycle. In this comprehensive discussion, we will explore the transition from linear to circular supply chains, examine the principles and benefits of circular economies, and identify strategies for reimagining supply chains to promote sustainability and resilience.

1. **Principles of Circular Economies:**

Circular economies are based on the principles of designing out waste, keeping products and materials in use, and regenerating natural systems. Unlike linear economies, which rely on a "take-make-dispose" model of production and consumption, circular economies aim to close the loop by recovering, repurposing, and recycling materials to create value in a continuous cycle.

Key principles of circular economies include:

 - **Design for longevity and durability**: Products are designed with a focus on durability, repairability, and recyclability to extend their lifespan and minimize waste.

 - **Embrace resource efficiency:** Resources are managed in a closed-loop system, where materials are reused, remanufactured, or recycled to preserve their value and minimize resource extraction.

 - **Foster collaboration and innovation:** Circular economies require collaboration across value chains, sectors, and stakeholders to redesign products, processes, and business models for sustainability.

- Engage consumers in circular behavior: Consumers are encouraged to adopt circular behaviors, such as sharing, renting, and repurposing products, to reduce consumption and waste.

2. Benefits of Circular Supply Chains:

Circular supply chains offer a wide range of environmental, economic, and social benefits for businesses, society, and the planet. By transitioning to circular economies, businesses can reduce their environmental footprint, improve resource efficiency, and enhance their resilience to supply chain disruptions. Moreover, circular supply chains can create new revenue streams, drive innovation, and foster collaboration across value chains. From reducing greenhouse gas emissions and conserving natural resources to creating jobs and promoting social inclusion, circular economies offer a holistic approach to sustainable development.

Key benefits of circular supply chains include:

- Waste reduction and resource conservation: Circular supply chains minimize waste generation, reduce the demand for virgin materials, and conserve natural resources, contributing to environmental sustainability.

- Cost savings and operational efficiency: By optimizing resource use, reducing waste, and improving process efficiency, circular supply chains can lower production costs, enhance profitability, and increase competitiveness.

- Innovation and value creation: Circular economies stimulate innovation in product design, material science, and business models, creating opportunities for new products, services, and markets.

- Resilience and risk mitigation: Circular supply chains are inherently more resilient to supply chain disruptions, such as raw material shortages, price fluctuations, and geopolitical instability, as they rely on diverse sources of materials and suppliers.

3. Strategies for Reimagining Supply Chains:

Transitioning to circular supply chains requires a strategic and holistic approach that encompasses product design, sourcing, production, distribution, and end-of-life management. Businesses can adopt a variety of strategies to reimagine their supply chains for sustainability and resilience.

Key strategies for reimagining supply chains include:

- **Designing for circularity:** Adopting principles of eco-design, such as modular design, material selection, and product lifecycle assessment, to minimize waste and maximize recyclability.

- **Implementing closed-loop systems:** Establishing reverse logistics, recycling infrastructure, and take-back programs to recover and repurpose materials at the end of their life cycle.

- **Collaborating with stakeholders:** Engaging suppliers, customers, regulators, and other stakeholders in collaborative partnerships to drive systemic change and promote circularity across value chains.

- **Leveraging technology and data:** Harnessing digital technologies, such as blockchain, Internet of Things (IoT), and artificial intelligence, to optimize supply chain visibility, traceability, and efficiency.

- **Educating and empowering consumers:** Raising awareness about circular economy principles and encouraging consumers to make informed choices that support sustainable consumption and circular behavior.

In conclusion, reimagining supply chains from linear to circular economies is essential for achieving environmental sustainability, economic prosperity, and social well-being. By embracing circular economy principles, businesses can create value, reduce waste, and foster resilience throughout their supply chains. From reducing environmental impacts and conserving resources to driving innovation and creating new growth opportunities, circular supply chains offer a pathway towards a more sustainable and resilient future for businesses and society. As businesses navigate the transition to circular economies, they have an opportunity to lead by example, inspire change, and make a positive impact on the planet and its inhabitants.

- Innovating for Sustainability: Harnessing Technology and Creativity

Innovation lies at the heart of sustainable development, offering transformative solutions to address complex environmental, social, and economic challenges. As the global community grapples with pressing issues such as climate change, resource depletion, social inequality, and economic volatility, there is an urgent need for businesses to harness the power of technology and creativity to drive sustainable innovation. In this comprehensive discussion, we will explore the role of innovation in advancing sustainability goals, examine the potential of technology and creativity to drive positive change and identify strategies for businesses to innovate sustainably and create lasting impact.

1. **The Role of Innovation in Sustainability:**

Innovation is essential for achieving sustainability goals by enabling businesses to develop new products, services, and business models that minimize environmental impact, promote social equity, and enhance economic prosperity. Sustainable innovation involves not only technological advancements but also organizational, cultural, and systemic changes that foster creativity, collaboration, and continuous improvement. By embracing a culture of innovation and investing in research, development, and experimentation, businesses can unlock new opportunities for growth, differentiation, and competitive advantage.

2. Harnessing Technology for Sustainability:

Technology plays a pivotal role in driving sustainable innovation by providing tools, solutions, and insights to address environmental and social challenges effectively. From renewable energy and clean technologies to digital platforms and data analytics, technology offers a myriad of opportunities to optimize resource use, reduce emissions, and improve efficiency across industries. Moreover, emerging technologies such as artificial intelligence, the Internet of Things (IoT), and blockchain have the potential to revolutionize sustainability by enhancing transparency, traceability, and accountability throughout supply chains and value networks.

Key areas where technology can drive sustainable innovation include:

- Renewable energy and energy efficiency: Leveraging solar, wind, and other renewable energy sources to reduce carbon emissions and transition towards a low-carbon economy.

- **Sustainable agriculture and food systems:** Using precision farming, agtech, and blockchain to enhance productivity, traceability, and transparency in food production and distribution.

- **Circular economy and waste management:** Implementing recycling, reuse, and remanufacturing technologies to minimize waste and maximize resource recovery in a closed-loop system.

- **Smart cities and sustainable mobility:** Developing smart infrastructure, transportation systems, and urban planning solutions to promote sustainable mobility, reduce congestion, and enhance quality of life.

3. **Fostering Creativity and Collaboration:**

Creativity is a catalyst for sustainable innovation, driving breakthroughs, and unconventional solutions to complex sustainability challenges. By fostering a culture of creativity, experimentation, and collaboration, businesses can inspire employees, engage stakeholders, and unlock untapped innovation potential. Moreover, collaboration across sectors, disciplines, and geographies is essential for tackling systemic issues and scaling up sustainable solutions.

Strategies for fostering creativity and collaboration include:

- **Creating spaces for ideation and experimentation:** Establishing innovation labs, incubators, and cross-functional teams to explore new ideas, prototype solutions, and test hypotheses.

- **Encouraging diversity and inclusion**: Embracing diverse perspectives, backgrounds, and experiences to foster creativity, innovation, and problem-solving.

- **Partnering with stakeholders:** Collaborating with customers, suppliers, academia, and civil society organizations to co-create solutions, share knowledge, and leverage collective expertise.

- **Investing in education and training:** Providing employees with opportunities for continuous learning, skill development, and creative thinking to cultivate an innovation mindset.

4. Scaling Up Sustainable Innovation:

Scaling up sustainable innovation requires a strategic and systematic approach that integrates innovation into core business strategies, processes, and systems. By aligning innovation efforts with sustainability goals, businesses can drive meaningful impact, create value for stakeholders, and contribute to a more sustainable and resilient future.

Strategies for scaling up sustainable innovation include:

- **Embedding sustainability into business strategies:** Integrating sustainability considerations into strategic planning, product development, and investment decisions to align innovation efforts with long-term sustainability goals.

- **Establishing metrics and benchmarks:** Developing key performance indicators (KPIs) and sustainability metrics to track progress, measure impact, and drive accountability for sustainable innovation.

- Leveraging networks and platforms:
Engaging with innovation ecosystems, industry alliances, and collaborative platforms to share best practices, access resources, and amplify impact through collective action.

- Communicating and celebrating success:
Sharing stories of sustainable innovation, highlighting achievements, and recognizing employees' contributions to inspire others and build momentum for change.

In conclusion, innovating for sustainability requires a concerted effort to harness the power of technology and creativity to drive positive change. By embracing a culture of innovation, investing in research and development, and collaborating with stakeholders, businesses can unlock new opportunities for growth, differentiation, and competitive advantage while advancing sustainability goals. As businesses navigate the transition towards a more sustainable future, they have an opportunity to lead by example, inspire change, and make a lasting impact on the planet and its inhabitants.

- Engaging Stakeholders: Building Trust and Collaboration

In the complex landscape of sustainable business practices, engaging stakeholders is paramount to building trust, fostering collaboration, and driving positive change. Stakeholders encompass a wide range of individuals, groups, and organizations that are impacted by or have an interest in a company's operations, products, and decisions. From employees and customers to investors, suppliers, communities, and civil society organizations, effective stakeholder engagement involves listening, understanding, and responding to diverse perspectives, needs, and expectations. In this comprehensive discussion, we will explore the importance of engaging stakeholders in sustainability efforts, examine the principles and benefits of stakeholder engagement, and identify strategies for businesses to build trust and collaboration with stakeholders.

1. Importance of Stakeholder Engagement in Sustainability:

Stakeholder engagement is integral to sustainability efforts as it enables businesses to identify risks, opportunities, and priorities, inform decision-making, and build legitimacy and support for sustainability initiatives. By involving stakeholders in the co-creation of solutions, businesses can enhance the relevance, credibility, and effectiveness of their sustainability strategies and initiatives. Moreover, stakeholder engagement fosters transparency, accountability, and trust, laying the foundation for long-term relationships and shared value creation.

2. Principles of Stakeholder Engagement:

Effective stakeholder engagement is guided by principles of inclusivity, transparency, responsiveness, and collaboration. It involves not only communication and consultation but also active participation, empowerment, and dialogue. By adopting a stakeholder-centric approach, businesses can create meaningful opportunities for stakeholders to contribute to decision-making processes, share insights and expertise, and co-design solutions that address their concerns and aspirations.

Key principles of stakeholder engagement include:

- **Inclusivity:** Ensuring representation and participation of diverse stakeholders, including marginalized and vulnerable groups, in decision-making processes.

- **Transparency:** Providing timely and accurate information about business activities, impacts, and performance to build trust and credibility with stakeholders.

- **Responsiveness:** Listening to stakeholder feedback, addressing concerns, and incorporating input into decision-making to demonstrate accountability and respect for stakeholder perspectives.

- **Collaboration:** Collaborating with stakeholders in a spirit of partnership and mutual respect to co-create solutions, share resources, and achieve shared goals.

3. Benefits of Stakeholder Engagement:

Stakeholder engagement offers a wide range of benefits for businesses, including enhanced risk management, improved decision-making, increased innovation, and enhanced reputation and brand value. By engaging with stakeholders, businesses can build social licenses to operate, anticipate and mitigate risks, and identify emerging opportunities for value creation. Moreover, stakeholder engagement fosters trust, loyalty, and brand advocacy among customers, employees, and other stakeholders, enhancing business resilience and competitiveness.

Key benefits of stakeholder engagement include:

- **Risk mitigation:** Identifying and addressing social, environmental, and governance risks through early engagement with stakeholders to prevent conflicts and reputational damage.

- **Innovation and creativity:** Tapping into diverse perspectives, knowledge, and expertise to drive innovation, creativity, and continuous improvement in products, services, and processes.

- **Reputation and brand enhancement:** Building trust, credibility, and loyalty among stakeholders through transparent communication, responsible business practices, and meaningful engagement.

- **Regulatory compliance and social license:** Demonstrating commitment to corporate social responsibility and sustainability goals to meet regulatory requirements, maintain social license to operate, and attract investment.

4. Strategies for Stakeholder Engagement:

Effective stakeholder engagement requires a strategic and systematic approach that integrates stakeholder perspectives into decision-making processes, governance structures, and performance management systems. By adopting best practices and leveraging technology, businesses can enhance the effectiveness and impact of their stakeholder engagement efforts.

Key strategies for stakeholder engagement include:

- Stakeholder mapping and analysis: Identifying and prioritizing stakeholders based on their level of influence, interest, and impact on business operations and sustainability issues.

- Tailored communication and outreach: Developing targeted communication strategies and channels to reach different stakeholder groups, taking into account their preferences, language, and cultural context.

- **Meaningful consultation and dialogue:**
Creating opportunities for two-way communication, dialogue, and feedback exchange with stakeholders through forums, consultations, surveys, and focus groups.

- **Collaboration and partnership building:**
Establishing collaborative partnerships with stakeholders, including industry peers, NGOs, government agencies, and academia, to address shared challenges and opportunities.

- **Continuous monitoring and evaluation:**
Monitoring stakeholder perceptions, feedback, and engagement levels over time and evaluating the effectiveness and impact of stakeholder engagement activities to inform continuous improvement.

In conclusion, engaging stakeholders is essential for building trust, fostering collaboration, and driving positive change in sustainability efforts. By adopting principles of inclusivity, transparency, responsiveness, and collaboration, businesses can create meaningful opportunities for stakeholders to contribute to decision-making processes, share insights and expertise, and co-create solutions that address shared challenges and opportunities. As businesses navigate the complexities of sustainability, they have an opportunity to lead by example, inspire change, and make a meaningful impact on the planet and its inhabitants through effective stakeholder engagement.

CHAPTER 4: CULTIVATING A PURPOSE-DRIVEN CULTURE

In the pursuit of sustainable business practices, cultivating a purpose-driven culture emerges as a cornerstone for organizations striving to navigate the complexities of the modern business landscape. A purpose-driven culture transcends mere profit maximization, anchoring the ethos of a company in a broader mission that serves society, the environment, and its stakeholders. It is a culture that inspires employees, galvanizes teams and guides decision-making towards creating meaningful impact beyond financial metrics.

In this chapter, we delve into the importance of cultivating a purpose-driven culture within organizations, exploring how it fosters employee engagement, drives innovation, and enables businesses to align their values with their actions. By weaving purpose into the fabric of organizational identity, companies can cultivate a sense of meaning and belonging among employees, fueling motivation and resilience in the face of challenges.

Throughout this discussion, we will examine the principles and practices that underpin purpose-driven cultures, drawing insights from pioneering organizations and thought leaders. From defining a compelling purpose statement to embedding purpose in leadership, operations, and employee experiences, we will explore the strategies for nurturing a culture that embraces sustainability, inclusivity, and ethical leadership.

As businesses strive to navigate an increasingly complex and interconnected world, cultivating a purpose-driven culture becomes not just a moral imperative but also a strategic imperative for long-term success. By aligning purpose with profit, organizations can unlock the full potential of their workforce, foster innovation, and create shared value for all stakeholders.

Join us as we embark on a journey to explore the transformative power of purpose-driven cultures, where passion meets purpose, and where businesses thrive not just for themselves but for the betterment of society and the planet. Welcome to "Cultivating a Purpose-Driven Culture"—where meaning meets momentum, and where the possibilities for positive change are limitless.

- Leadership in the Age of Sustainability: Inspiring Vision and Driving Change

In the contemporary landscape of business and society, leadership plays a pivotal role in shaping the trajectory towards sustainability. Leaders are not only responsible for setting strategic direction and driving organizational performance but also for inspiring a vision of a more sustainable and equitable future. In this comprehensive discussion, we will explore the role of leadership in advancing sustainability goals, examine the attributes and behaviors of effective sustainability leaders, and identify strategies for inspiring vision and driving change in the age of sustainability.

1. **The Role of Leadership in Sustainability:**

Leadership is essential for driving sustainability initiatives and embedding sustainability principles into the DNA of organizations. Sustainable leaders are visionary, strategic, and collaborative, with a deep understanding of the interconnectedness of social, environmental, and economic issues. They inspire others to embrace sustainability as a core value and guide organizations towards achieving long-term sustainability goals while balancing the interests of stakeholders.

2. **Attributes of Effective Sustainability Leaders:**

Effective sustainability leaders possess a unique set of attributes and competencies that enable them to navigate the complexities of sustainability challenges and opportunities. These attributes include:

- **Visionary leadership:** Inspiring a compelling vision of a sustainable future and mobilizing stakeholders towards its realization.

- **Strategic thinking:** Developing and implementing sustainability strategies that align with organizational goals and create value for stakeholders.

- **Collaboration and stakeholder engagement:** Building partnerships and fostering dialogue with stakeholders to co-create solutions and drive collective action.

- **Systems thinking:** Understanding the interconnectedness of social, environmental, and economic systems and identifying leverage points for sustainable change.

- **Resilience and adaptability:** Navigating uncertainty and ambiguity, embracing change, and learning from setbacks to drive continuous improvement.

- **Ethical and values-based leadership:** Demonstrating integrity, transparency, and ethical conduct in decision-making and operations, and aligning actions with organizational values.

3. **Strategies for Inspiring Vision and Driving Change:**

Inspiring vision and driving change towards sustainability requires a strategic and systematic approach that engages stakeholders, fosters innovation, and embeds sustainability into organizational culture and practices. Leaders can adopt the following strategies to inspire vision and drive change:

- **Articulating a compelling sustainability vision:** Communicating a clear and inspiring vision of sustainability that resonates with stakeholders and aligns with organizational purpose and values.

- **Setting ambitious goals and targets:** Establishing measurable sustainability goals and targets that drive progress, accountability, and continuous improvement.

- **Empowering and enabling employees:** Fostering a culture of innovation, collaboration, and empowerment that encourages employees to contribute ideas, take ownership, and drive sustainability initiatives.

- **Leading by example:** Modeling sustainable behaviors and practices, demonstrating a commitment to sustainability goals, and inspiring others to follow suit.

- **Building coalitions and partnerships:** Collaborating with industry peers, governments, NGOs, and other stakeholders to leverage resources, share best practices, and drive systemic change.

- **Embedding sustainability into governance and decision-making:** Integrating sustainability considerations into governance structures, performance metrics, and decision-making processes to ensure alignment with organizational goals and values.

- Investing in leadership development: Providing training, coaching, and mentorship opportunities to develop the next generation of sustainability leaders and build leadership capacity across the organization.

In conclusion, leadership in the age of sustainability requires a transformative mindset, visionary leadership, and a commitment to driving positive change. By inspiring vision, fostering collaboration, and driving innovation, sustainability leaders can navigate the complexities of sustainability challenges and opportunities and create a more sustainable and equitable future for all. As businesses and society grapple with urgent sustainability issues, the role of leadership becomes more critical than ever in charting a course towards a thriving, resilient, and sustainable world.

Fostering Employee Engagement: Empowering Teams and Nurturing Talent

Employee engagement is a cornerstone of organizational success, driving productivity, innovation, and resilience. In the context of sustainability, engaged employees are critical allies in driving positive change, as they are more likely to embrace sustainability goals, contribute innovative ideas, and champion sustainability initiatives within their organizations. In this comprehensive discussion, we will explore the importance of fostering employee engagement in sustainability efforts, examine the factors that influence employee engagement, and identify strategies for empowering teams and nurturing talent to drive sustainability forward.

1. **Importance of Employee Engagement in Sustainability:**

Employee engagement is essential for the success of sustainability initiatives, as engaged employees are more committed, motivated, and aligned with organizational goals and values. Engaged employees are also more likely to embrace sustainability as a core value and actively contribute to sustainability efforts through their work, behavior, and decision-making. Moreover, engaged employees are more resilient to change, more innovative, and more likely to advocate for sustainability both inside and outside the organization.

2. **Factors Influencing Employee Engagement:**

Employee engagement is influenced by a wide range of factors, including leadership, organizational culture, job design, communication, recognition, and development opportunities. Sustainable organizations prioritize employee well-being, inclusion, and empowerment, creating a work environment where employees feel valued, respected, and motivated to contribute their best. Factors that influence employee engagement in sustainability efforts include:

- **Leadership commitment:** Leadership plays a critical role in setting the tone for sustainability and creating a culture of engagement and accountability.

- **Organizational culture:** A culture that values sustainability, fosters collaboration, and encourages open communication enhances employee engagement in sustainability efforts.

- **Clear purpose and values:** Employees are more engaged when they understand and connect with the organization's purpose, values, and sustainability goals.

- **Meaningful work:** Providing opportunities for employees to contribute to meaningful sustainability projects and initiatives enhances their sense of purpose and engagement.

- **Opportunities for growth and development:** Investing in employee training, development, and career advancement opportunities fosters engagement and retention.

- **Recognition and rewards:** Recognizing and rewarding employees for their contributions to sustainability reinforces positive behavior and fosters a sense of pride and ownership.

3. Strategies for Empowering Teams and Nurturing Talent:

Empowering teams and nurturing talent is essential for fostering employee engagement in sustainability efforts. Organizations can adopt a variety of strategies to empower employees, nurture talent, and create a culture of engagement and innovation:

- **Provide training and development opportunities:** Invest in employee training and development programs to build skills, knowledge, and capabilities related to sustainability.

- **Foster a culture of collaboration and innovation:** Create opportunities for cross-functional collaboration, idea-sharing, and innovation to empower employees to contribute their ideas and expertise to sustainability efforts.

- Encourage employee participation and involvement: Involve employees in decision-making processes, project teams, and sustainability initiatives to foster a sense of ownership and commitment.

- Communicate transparently and regularly: Keep employees informed about sustainability goals, progress, and challenges through transparent communication channels, such as town halls, newsletters, and intranet portals.

- Provide resources and support: Provide employees with the tools, resources, and support they need to engage in sustainability efforts effectively, such as access to data, training, and mentorship.

- Recognize and reward sustainability achievements: Acknowledge and celebrate employees' contributions to sustainability through recognition programs, awards, and incentives.

- **Lead by example:** Demonstrate leadership commitment to sustainability through visible actions, such as participating in sustainability initiatives, incorporating sustainability into performance evaluations, and holding leaders accountable for sustainability goals.

In conclusion, fostering employee engagement is essential for driving sustainability forward and creating a culture of innovation, collaboration, and accountability. By empowering teams, nurturing talent, and creating a supportive work environment, organizations can harness the full potential of their employees to advance sustainability goals and create a positive impact. As businesses and society grapple with urgent sustainability challenges, engaged employees are essential allies in building a more sustainable and equitable future for all.

- Ethical Governance: Setting Standards and Upholding Integrity

Ethical governance forms the bedrock of sustainable and responsible business practices, encompassing the principles, values, and standards that guide organizational decision-making, conduct, and accountability. In an era marked by increasing scrutiny of corporate behavior and the growing recognition of the interconnectedness between business, society, and the environment, ethical governance is essential for building trust, mitigating risks, and fostering long-term sustainability. In this comprehensive discussion, we will explore the importance of ethical governance in driving sustainable business practices, examine the key components of ethical governance frameworks, and identify strategies for setting standards and upholding integrity within organizations.

1. Importance of Ethical Governance in Sustainability:

Ethical governance is integral to sustainability, as it ensures that organizations operate in a manner that is transparent, accountable, and aligned with ethical principles and values. Ethical governance guides decision-making processes, shapes organizational culture, and informs stakeholder relationships, fostering trust and confidence among stakeholders. Moreover, ethical governance helps organizations identify and mitigate risks, prevent misconduct, and enhance reputation and brand value, contributing to long-term sustainability and success.

2. Key Components of Ethical Governance Frameworks:

Ethical governance frameworks encompass a set of principles, policies, and practices that guide ethical conduct and decision-making within organizations. While specific components may vary depending on the nature and size of the organization, key elements of ethical governance frameworks include:

- **Code of ethics and conduct:** Establishing a code of ethics that articulates the organization's values, principles, and standards of behavior, and providing guidance on ethical decision-making and conduct.

- **Compliance with laws and regulations:** Ensuring compliance with applicable laws, regulations, and industry standards, and adopting internal controls and processes to monitor and enforce compliance.

- **Transparency and disclosure:** Providing transparent and accurate information about the organization's operations, performance, and governance practices to stakeholders, including investors, employees, customers, and the public.

- **Accountability and oversight:** Establishing mechanisms for oversight, accountability, and reporting, such as governance structures, board committees, and internal audit functions, to ensure effective governance and risk management.

- Stakeholder engagement: Engaging with stakeholders, including employees, customers, suppliers, and communities, to understand their expectations, address concerns, and incorporate their perspectives into decision-making processes.

- Risk management and mitigation: Identifying, assessing, and managing risks related to ethical conduct, integrity, and reputation, and implementing controls and processes to mitigate risks effectively.

- Continuous improvement: Committing to ongoing monitoring, evaluation, and improvement of ethical governance practices through periodic reviews, assessments, and feedback mechanisms.

3. **Strategies for Setting Standards and Upholding Integrity:**

Upholding integrity and setting high ethical standards requires a proactive and systematic approach that involves leadership commitment, organizational culture, and accountability mechanisms. Organizations can adopt a variety of strategies to promote ethical governance and uphold integrity:

- **Leadership commitment:** Demonstrate visible and unwavering commitment to ethical governance from senior leadership, including the board of directors, CEO, and executive management team.

- **Embed ethics into organizational culture:** Foster a culture of integrity, transparency, and accountability by promoting ethical values, behaviors, and decision-making throughout the organization.

- **Provide ethics training and education:** Offer ethics training and education programs to employees at all levels to raise awareness of ethical issues, build ethical decision-making skills, and reinforce the importance of integrity.

- **Implement robust policies and procedures:** Develop and implement comprehensive policies and procedures that govern ethical conduct, including codes of conduct, whistleblower policies, conflict of interest policies, and anti-corruption measures.

- Establish oversight and accountability mechanisms: Create governance structures, committees, and processes to oversee and monitor compliance with ethical standards, and hold individuals accountable for unethical behavior through disciplinary measures when necessary.

- Encourage reporting and whistleblowing: Establish confidential reporting channels, such as hotlines or anonymous reporting systems, to encourage employees to report ethical concerns or misconduct without fear of retaliation.

- Conduct regular audits and assessments: Conduct periodic audits and assessments of ethical governance practices to identify areas for improvement, address gaps, and ensure ongoing compliance with ethical standards.

In conclusion, ethical governance is essential for driving sustainable business practices, fostering trust, and creating value for all stakeholders. By setting high standards, upholding integrity, and promoting a culture of ethics and accountability, organizations can mitigate risks, build reputation and brand value, and contribute to long-term sustainability and success. As businesses navigate the complexities of the modern world, ethical governance serves as a guiding principle that ensures organizations operate with integrity, transparency, and responsibility, thereby creating a positive impact on society, the environment, and future generations.

CHAPTER 5: NAVIGATING THE FUTURE OF SUSTAINABLE BUSINESS

In an era marked by unprecedented global challenges, from climate change and resource depletion to social inequality and economic uncertainty, the imperative for sustainable business practices has never been more pressing. As businesses navigate the complexities of an ever-changing landscape, the future of sustainable business emerges as a pivotal focal point. In this chapter, we embark on a journey to explore the emerging trends, opportunities, and challenges shaping the future of sustainable business.

The landscape of sustainable business is rapidly evolving, driven by shifting consumer preferences, regulatory changes, technological advancements, and growing stakeholder expectations. As organizations seek to future-proof their operations and create long-term value, they are increasingly integrating sustainability into their core business strategies, operations, and culture. This chapter serves as a guide for businesses seeking to navigate the road ahead, offering insights, perspectives, and strategies to thrive in the age of sustainability.

Throughout this discussion, we will examine the key trends and drivers shaping the future of sustainable business, from the rise of stakeholder capitalism and the circular economy to the increasing focus on social impact and ethical governance. We will explore how businesses can seize opportunities for innovation, collaboration, and leadership in driving positive change, while also addressing the risks and challenges that lie ahead.

As we navigate the future of sustainable business, it is essential to recognize that sustainability is not just a goal to be achieved but a journey to be embraced. By embracing sustainability as a strategic imperative and adopting a holistic approach to business innovation and transformation, organizations can create value for all stakeholders while contributing to a more sustainable, equitable, and prosperous future for generations to come.

Join us as we embark on a journey to explore the future of sustainable business—a future where purpose meets profit, where innovation meets impact, and where businesses lead the way towards a more sustainable and resilient world. Welcome to "Navigating the Future of Sustainable Business," where the possibilities are limitless, and the opportunities for positive change are boundless.

- Anticipating Trends and Disruptions: The Role of Scenario Planning

In today's rapidly changing business landscape, characterized by technological advancements, geopolitical shifts, and evolving consumer preferences, organizations face a multitude of uncertainties and disruptions. Anticipating future trends and disruptions is crucial for businesses to proactively adapt, innovate, and thrive in an increasingly complex and volatile environment. Scenario planning emerges as a powerful tool for organizations to systematically explore alternative futures, assess risks and opportunities, and develop resilient strategies to navigate uncertainty. In this comprehensive discussion, we will explore the role of scenario planning in anticipating trends and disruptions, examine best practices for scenario planning, and identify strategies for applying scenario planning in business decision-making.

1. **Understanding Scenario Planning:**

Scenario planning is a strategic foresight methodology that involves creating a set of plausible future scenarios to explore the range of potential outcomes and their implications for the organization. Unlike traditional forecasting methods, which rely on extrapolating past trends or predicting a single future outcome, scenario planning embraces uncertainty and complexity by considering multiple possible futures and their underlying drivers. By identifying key uncertainties and their potential impacts, organizations can develop robust strategies that are flexible, adaptive, and resilient to change.

2. **The Role of Scenario Planning in Anticipating Trends and Disruptions:**

Scenario planning plays a critical role in helping organizations anticipate trends and disruptions by:

- **Exploring alternative futures:** Scenario planning enables organizations to systematically explore a range of possible futures, including best-case, worst-case, and most likely scenarios, based on different combinations of critical uncertainties.

- **Identifying early warning signals**: By analyzing signals of change and weak signals from the external environment, scenario planning helps organizations identify emerging trends, disruptions, and discontinuities before they fully manifest.

- **Assessing risks and opportunities:** Scenario planning allows organizations to assess the potential risks and opportunities associated with different future scenarios, enabling them to develop proactive strategies to mitigate risks and capitalize on opportunities.

- **Challenging assumptions and mental models:** Scenario planning challenges organizations to question their existing assumptions, mental models, and strategic plans, fostering a culture of innovation, learning, and adaptability.

- **Enhancing strategic decision-making:** By providing a structured framework for considering alternative futures and their implications, scenario planning helps organizations make more informed, forward-looking strategic decisions that are aligned with their long-term goals and objectives.

3. Best Practices for Scenario Planning:

To effectively anticipate trends and disruptions through scenario planning, organizations can adopt the following best practices:

- **Define the scope and objectives:** Clearly define the scope and objectives of the scenario planning exercise, including the key uncertainties and drivers of change to be considered.

- **Engage diverse perspectives:** Involve stakeholders from across the organization, including senior leadership, subject matter experts, and frontline employees, to bring diverse perspectives and insights to the scenario planning process.

- **Conduct robust analysis:** Use a combination of qualitative and quantitative methods to analyze the drivers of change, assess their potential impacts, and develop plausible future scenarios.

- **Develop narrative scenarios:** Create narrative scenarios that describe the plausible futures in rich detail, including the key events, trends, and interactions that shape each scenario.

- **Test assumptions and implications:** Test the underlying assumptions and implications of each scenario through scenario workshops, tabletop exercises, or simulation exercises to identify blind spots and gaps in understanding.

- **Monitor and update regularly:** Continuously monitor changes in the external environment, update scenarios as new information becomes available, and refine strategies accordingly to ensure relevance and effectiveness.

4. **Applying Scenario Planning in Business Decision-Making:**

Scenario planning can be applied across various areas of business decision-making, including strategic planning, risk management, innovation, and contingency planning. Organizations can use scenario planning to:

- **Inform strategic priorities and investments:** Use scenario planning to identify emerging opportunities and threats, prioritize strategic initiatives, and allocate resources effectively.

- **Enhance risk management:** Anticipate potential risks and disruptions, develop contingency plans, and build resilience to withstand unforeseen events and shocks.

- **Foster innovation and agility:** Stimulate creative thinking, explore alternative business models, and identify new growth opportunities in response to changing market dynamics and customer needs.

- **Support long-term sustainability:** Incorporate sustainability considerations into scenario planning to anticipate future trends, assess the environmental and social impacts of different scenarios, and develop strategies that promote sustainable growth and resilience.

In conclusion, scenario planning is a valuable tool for organizations seeking to anticipate trends and disruptions, build resilience, and thrive in an uncertain and rapidly changing world. By embracing uncertainty, exploring alternative futures, and developing proactive strategies, organizations can position themselves to navigate future challenges and capitalize on emerging opportunities. As businesses increasingly recognize the importance of strategic foresight and resilience, scenario planning will continue to play a vital role in shaping the future of sustainable business and driving positive change.

- Scaling Impact: From Local Initiatives to Global Movements

In the realm of sustainable business, scaling impact is crucial for addressing pressing global challenges and driving meaningful change. While local initiatives play a vital role in driving innovation and creating a positive impact at the grassroots level, scaling these initiatives to a global level is essential for achieving widespread, systemic change. In this comprehensive discussion, we will explore the importance of scaling impact in sustainable business, examine strategies for scaling local initiatives to global movements, and identify key success factors and challenges in the process.

1. Importance of Scaling Impact in Sustainable Business:

Scaling impact is essential for maximizing the effectiveness and reach of sustainable business initiatives. While local initiatives may deliver meaningful results within specific communities or regions, scaling these initiatives to a global level enables organizations to address systemic issues, leverage economies of scale, and create transformative change on a broader scale. By scaling impact, organizations can amplify their positive contributions to environmental conservation, social equity, and economic development, while also fostering innovation, collaboration, and learning across borders and sectors.

2. Strategies for Scaling Local Initiatives to Global Movements:

Scaling local initiatives to global movements requires a strategic and systematic approach that involves collaboration, innovation, and collective action. Organizations can adopt various strategies to scale impact effectively:

- **Partnership and collaboration:** Forge strategic partnerships and alliances with like-minded organizations, governments, and civil society organizations to pool resources, share expertise, and amplify impact.

- **Empowerment and capacity building:** Empower local communities, organizations, and grassroots leaders to take ownership of initiatives and drive change from the bottom up.

- **Leveraging technology and innovation:** Harness the power of technology, digital platforms, and innovation to scale solutions, reach new audiences, and enhance efficiency and effectiveness.

- **Advocacy and policy influence:** Advocate for policy reforms, regulatory changes, and international agreements that support sustainable development goals and create an enabling environment for scaling impact.

- **Scaling models and replication:** Identify successful models and best practices from local initiatives and replicate them in new contexts, adapting them to local needs and conditions.

- **Mobilizing resources and funding:** Mobilize financial resources, grants, investments, and philanthropic support to scale initiatives and sustain long-term impact.

- **Building networks and communities of practice:** Establish networks, communities of practice, and knowledge-sharing platforms to connect stakeholders, facilitate learning, and exchange insights and experiences.

3. **Key Success Factors and Challenges:**

While scaling impact offers immense opportunities for driving positive change, it also presents several challenges and complexities. Key success factors for scaling impact include:

- **Leadership and vision:** Strong leadership, vision, and commitment are essential for mobilizing stakeholders, fostering collaboration, and driving collective action towards shared goals.

- **Adaptability and flexibility:** Flexibility and adaptability are critical for responding to changing circumstances, evolving needs, and unforeseen challenges during the scaling process.

- **Measurement and evaluation:** Robust monitoring, evaluation, and learning mechanisms are necessary for tracking progress, measuring impact, and refining strategies for scaling impact.

- **Inclusivity and equity:** Ensuring inclusivity, diversity, and equity in the scaling process are essential for addressing power imbalances, reducing inequalities, and maximizing social impact.

- **Sustainability and resilience:** Building resilience and ensuring the long-term sustainability of scaled initiatives require careful planning, resource allocation, and risk management.

Challenges in scaling impact include:

- **Resource constraints:** Limited funding, capacity, and expertise can hinder efforts to scale impact, requiring organizations to be resourceful and innovative in their approach.

- **Complexity and fragmentation:** Scaling impact in complex, fragmented systems requires navigating diverse stakeholders, interests, and agendas, often requiring patience, diplomacy, and compromise.

- **Resistance to change:** Resistance to change from vested interests, entrenched systems, and cultural norms can impede efforts to scale impact, necessitating effective communication, advocacy, and stakeholder engagement.

- **Unintended consequences:** Scaling impact can sometimes lead to unintended consequences or negative externalities, such as displacement of local communities or environmental degradation, highlighting the importance of careful planning and risk assessment.

In conclusion, scaling impact from local initiatives to global movements is essential for achieving widespread, transformative change in sustainable business. By leveraging partnerships, innovation, and collective action, organizations can amplify their positive contributions, address systemic issues, and create a more sustainable, equitable, and prosperous future for all. As businesses and society increasingly recognize the urgency and importance of scaling impact, the need for strategic foresight, collaboration, and leadership in scaling sustainable initiatives will continue to grow.

CONCLUSION

In "The Thriving Vision: Charting the Path to Sustainable Business Success," we embarked on a journey to explore the transformative power of sustainable business practices and the imperative for organizations to embrace a thriving vision for the future. Throughout these pages, we have delved into the multifaceted dimensions of sustainability, from environmental stewardship and social responsibility to economic resilience and ethical governance, recognizing that sustainable business success requires a holistic approach that balances profit with purpose.

As we conclude our exploration, it is clear that the challenges facing businesses and society are complex and interconnected, requiring bold action, innovation, and collaboration to address. However, amidst these challenges lie tremendous opportunities for businesses to lead the way in driving positive change, creating value for all stakeholders, and contributing to a more sustainable and equitable world.

The journey towards sustainable business success is not without its obstacles, but it is a journey worth undertaking—a journey that holds the promise of a brighter future for generations to come. By charting a course guided by the principles of sustainability, organizations can unlock new opportunities for innovation, resilience, and prosperity, while also fulfilling their responsibility to society, the environment, and future generations.

As we look to the future, let us continue to nurture the thriving vision that has guided us on this journey—a vision of businesses that thrive not only financially but also socially, environmentally, and ethically. Let us continue to collaborate, innovate, and inspire one another to create a world where businesses serve as forces for good, where purpose drives profit, and where sustainability is not just a goal to be achieved but a way of life.

Thank you for joining us on this journey. May "The Thriving Vision" catalyze change, a source of inspiration, and a roadmap for businesses seeking to chart a path to sustainable success. Together, let us continue to chart the path towards a future where business thrives, communities flourish, and the planet prospers for generations to come.

www.ingramcontent.com/pod-product-compliance
Lightning Source LLC
Chambersburg PA
CBHW070152230526
45471CB00002B/627